TO PEOPLE PLEASE OR NOT, THAT IS THE QUESTION

THE UNCOMMON APPROACH TO HEALING AND UNVEILING THE ONLY LIGHT THAT MATTERS

VICTORIA TRAN

Dedication

To the team at Transcendent Publishing for helping me finish this beautiful passion project. Shanda and Mary made completing this beautiful project so easy and supported my vision so wholesomely that I could not ask for better help. I am so grateful to them for helping me see this through to the end!

Table of Contents

"Be a first-rate version of yourself, not a second-rate version of someone else."

–Judy Garland

Author's Note

Many times in my life, I was told that I should write a book. During those times, I would laugh it off because I couldn't imagine doing such a thing. It was so foreign, and I was afraid if I started writing it, I would stop due to a lack of motivation. In recent times, though, I found myself compelled. You can call it a writer's motivation or inspiration; however, it felt like the universe and all my guides came to me, and this book was the birth of that inspiration.

I want to give you a fair warning, though: this book is not for the faint of heart. The contents were poured from my heart directly to yours. It is my highest hope that you will understand it the way I did during my decade-long journey of self-acceptance, love, and forgiveness.

May these lessons help you during your darkest hours and unholiest moments, as books did for me when I was a young teenager who used to stay up late reading to quell the pain that plagued my heart. I want to remind you that someone out there can truly understand you. I can understand your pain, your trials, and your hurdles, and feeling like the world is against you. There were moments when I struggled to wake up and go about my day because the weight of being responsible, strong, and capable was just too much for me to bear.

I hope this reaches you at a point in your life that needs a flicker of hope. May it help guide your way in the dark when everything else seems to fade away because there is nothing else but you there …

It may be daunting and scary, but I promise that there is true happiness and self-acceptance on the other side. I hope that the thought of being you is more wonderful than you could ever have imagined, that waking up will finally feel like the reward and the blessing it is, and that everything you went through will mean something.

You are more precious than you believe. You are greater than you give yourself credit for. You mean so much to this world and to me, too. I don't need to see you physically to know you exist. You are accepting my heart as you read this book, and I thank you for that. I see you. I feel your pain. I see your truths. I believe in your challenges. More importantly, I believe that you are capable of seeing the light at the end of the tunnel as well.

Please know that you aren't alone and that you have another soul out there who does understand.

Thank you for reading this book when you needed it.

Introduction

"Treasure yourself because there is no one else to do it for you …"

—Victoria Tran

Hello friend!

I am glad you decided to read my hard-learned lessons from my years of pleasing people. There are many reasons why you decided to read this book. Regardless of the reason, I am so glad that you are here. You will read real stories about how my people-pleasing ways destroyed and rebirthed me. Dramatic? Absolutely! Ridiculous? Perhaps. After all, I was a huge fiction reader at one point in my life. I will surely deliver some drama here and there for reference as well.

For you to read this book right now means that, on some level, you know what it feels like to wear a mask. A mask that you hide behind when everyone is watching. It hides the constant fear that someone will see the real you underneath. The sad, broken, and not-so-perfect you that desperately wishes someone would understand and still love you no matter what ugliness arises.

Also, this book was meant for you to learn through my stories, relate if you wish, and see how you can start the small changes now. It was written in a workbook style because it was important that you know this is not about my journey. This is *your* story.

The moment you took on this book, you already knew that something had to change. That change has to be you ... because once you change, you can finally feel what it means to live in the best ways possible.

I want you to really understand the lessons. These are all hard-learned lessons that I came to later in life. I want you to apply them in a way that fits your life and what truly aligns with you. Why? Because you are *YOU*! No one else can be you, and no one after will ever be you. Only you can light up the way you can and, in turn, inspire others along the way.

Before starting, there are two things I would like to note. First, I am an embodiment coach. Everything written here helps you connect with your body's emotions and sensations. This is not a thought process, although I know it will be very stimulating. I invite you to feel into the different sensations that arise while reading the book. Take a moment to pause and softly observe them. Pay close attention and allow it to unfold naturally, without thoughts or arguments. You were meant to feel every moment of your life, for better and worse. The discomfort and resistance you feel from wanting to sit still with yourself is a testament to the traumas that imprinted on you and times of long past.

I am here to tell you that everything that happened to you is completely healable, but first, you need to accept yourself. I am not talking about just going to therapy and any other amazing modalities. I am talking about *you*. This is a book about your relationship with yourself. Can you allow yourself to *feel* any memories, thoughts, and emotions that come through without judgment or argument? This is not a blame game, either. It is not about who the victim was and who the victor is.

This is about learning to come home into yourself. Being comfortable with not feeling and being perfect all the time. Being comfortable with the idea that you may never get what you want. Being safe and content with the idea that everything really is working out in your favor, whether it feels like it or not. This is your story of faith, love, trust, and acceptance of yourself ... and it will be a spectacular one. I just know it.

Secondly, there was a playlist that I used to write this book. I invite you to listen to them for each chapter if you would like some help getting deeper into the work. Below is the chart I created to show you which pieces were used as inspiration for the chapters. They are all free to listen to on YouTube.

Without further ado, let's get going on this book. I was never one to write a lot!

	Intro	1	2	3	4	5	6	Conclusion
"Space" - French Fuse	X	X	X	X	X	X	X	X
"Your Dreams Are Incredibly Loud Tonight"–Mustafa Avsaroglu	X	X	X	X				
"Quiet Resource"– Evelyn Stein		X	X	X				
"Now We Are Free"– Jacob's Piano			X	X				X
"In This Moment"– Gavin Luke					X	X	X	
"The Gift"–Gavin Luke	X			X				X
"Where Spirits Sleep"–Eric Heitmann & Amy Wallace	X				X	X	X	X
"Invincible"–Jurrivh	X				X	X	X	X
"Hopeful"–BigRice-Piano	X	X	X					
"Find a Melody" (Slowed) Andrea Vanzo	X							
"Glimpse" (Slowed & Reverb) Gabriel Albuquerque	X						X	

LESSON ONE:

You Are Who You Are and Not the Image in Your Head

In our current world, everyone encourages us to "think" about who we want to be when we grow up. I am sure you have been asked at least once or twice the age-old questions, "What do you want to be when you grow up?" or "Who do you want to be like when you grow up?" The idea of us not knowing the answer, or worse, saying an unacceptable response, is too much for adults.

Throughout my childhood, I was asked these questions often. My answers went from a teacher to an archaeologist and even a circus performer. Needless to say, I caused my mother a lot of heartache and disappointment. Despite this, I was really proud of my mini-me. She had the courage to say the things that I, later in life, could not.

My family, like many others, had very high expectations of me. The rage was for a doctor or lawyer to join the home. Yet, my heart always drove me to wilder dreams like being a business owner, the President, or in the military.

When I was around 12 years old, I remember my older sister asking me what I would do when I turned 18. I succinctly said that I was going to join the military. She laughed at me and said I wouldn't do that because it's too hard, and I am too "weak" to do something like that. Against the odds, I joined the armed forces at 18, much to my family's displeasure. I guess this is where the sarcastic statement, "I aim to please … " comes from.

Around this time, I started realizing that I wanted to be someone special, someone important. I had a faint hope that if I became famous and important, then maybe, just maybe, I would be worthy of love, acceptance, and even attention from my family. My longing for these things was so deep that I did not think twice when I joined the military. To satisfy my dire need for love, I embarked on a journey to make my dreams come true.

What were those dreams, you ask? Simple. I dreamed of being an incredibly beautiful woman dressed in the most fashionable blue suit and a white shirt. Her feet wore the coolest heels, and she was someone important. She was talking to another important person on the phone while staring out a huge window that overlooked the city skyline. In this dream, that woman was me. I chased this image every day and every night. All my wishes and hopes were to become this woman. One could even call me obsessed with this dream.

For years, I chased and chased her. Every moment became harder than the last, and eventually, all my waking moments felt dull. My body began to feel incredibly heavy as I hunched over from the enormity of the dream. Even when I did rewarding work in the government, I dreaded going in every day because of the weight I felt. I can't begin to count how many nights I cried myself to sleep, feeling so desperately lonely and afraid. There were so many nights when I would be in my bedroom with just a lamp light, crying and wondering if I would ever become that amazing lady in my head.

But no matter what I did, I never felt closer to her. It hurt so much that she was right there, but I could not reach her. Despair doesn't seem to cover how I felt back then, but it is a good measure of what I experienced.

While I was in bed, crying my eyes out, it felt like everyone else was enjoying their lives, hanging out, drinking, and engaging in all sorts of fun. Despite knowing that it all came down to a choice, I just couldn't bring myself to choose fun. I was too "busy." Busy becoming this fantastical woman in my head who could possibly rule the world.

Just kidding.

The part that isn't a joke, though, is it conveys how much I sacrificed to become this woman in my head: the late nights and ridiculous amount of stress I endured for work, the many times I refused to fly home to visit my family because I was "too busy." All my simple values started to slip away, and I didn't even mind it. Why? Because I chose to chase after the woman in my head. She was my dream. She was important to me, and I thought that once I reached her, I would have everything I ever wanted.

The saddest part of this story is that I did become that woman. Eventually, I came to work for a tech company in downtown Austin. I got to wear my fancy suits and heels while overseeing an office. I was so busy on the phone or around the office that I didn't even prioritize my lunches or breaks. There were long and grueling days, but I was able to accomplish it all because I was the woman of my dreams! I was important! Everyone needed me, and I was always happy to oblige them. It didn't matter the time or place. I was always on the clock working to make everything and everyone look perfect.

That's when it hit me …

I was slaving away for an office that only knew how to ask me when they would get their food. No one ever asked me how I was doing. Even when I went through a traumatic breakup, not many asked me if I was doing okay. One of the employees later confessed that they suspected something was wrong but was confident that I would "get over it" eventually. It was so hard on me that I literally broke down while working at an event, yet I still couldn't comprehend what I was doing to myself. By pleasing others, no one ever turned around to please me.

Let's get factual for a moment. I do not want you to believe my workplace was horrible. It was not. They were great people. However, I never gave them an opening to please or help me. This is the result of chasing the woman in my head. She was so "perfect" that the idea of needing help was something foreign. She was me, and I was her, but that did not give me permission to adopt her and create nothing for myself.

The fact that I couldn't even enjoy my dream is wild enough. However, the worst part was how I sabotaged this wonderful dream. That is something we will cover in later lessons, though.

In the meantime, I would like you to reflect on this story, and ask yourself how you can relate. On the next page, you will see some questions to help you with this process if that is what you wish. After all, you are here to learn whether or not you need to people please. The best way to find out is to dig for the answers within yourself! I highly recommend trying it out and seeing what comes back.

Lesson One Questions

Now, I want to ask you some questions. Why? Because this is how you will learn why this lesson is significant for you. So, feel free to write in this section or on a separate piece of paper, and answer the following questions:

1. Who or what are you chasing? It could be a man/woman/partner, a dream, or a goal.

. . . .

. . . .

. . . .

. . . .

2. What makes you feel like you need to become or have that person/dream/goal to be fulfilled?

. . . .

. . . .

. . . .

. . . .

3. Imagine yourself having that unattainable person/dream/goal.

   a. Are you happy?

. . . .

. . . .

. . . .

. . . .

b. What are you doing?

. . . .

. . . .

. . . .

. . . .

c. How long are you excited for?

. . . .

. . . .

. . . .

. . . .

d. Does anyone wait for you when you come home?

. . . .

. . . .

. . . .

. . . .

e. What does that feel like?

. . . .

. . . .

. . . .

. . . .

f. Where do you relax?

. . . .

. . . .

. . . .

g. Who are you enjoying your time off with?

. . . .

. . . .

. . . .

. . . .

h. Is anyone supporting you in this dream or goal?

. . . .

. . . .

. . . .

. . . .

4. Why are you so desperate to have this person/dream/goal?

. . . .

. . . .

. . . .

. . . .

5. What are you missing that makes this person/dream/goal so fantastic?

. . . .

. . . .

. . . .

. . . .

Now save these answers for later!

We Are What We Feel, Not What We Think

For you to come across this book, I am almost positive that most of you have heard, "You need to think on the bright side," "Think happy thoughts ..." or perhaps, "Stop being a Debbie Downer." Sadly, many are under the assumption that as long as we "think" better, we will have better. Now, I would not discount this method. However, to arrive there, we must understand something ...

You need to remember that behind closed doors when the lights turn off, your thoughts can be your worst enemies. In your darkest hours, your brain can shout:

"How could I forget something so simple?"

"What is wrong with me?"

"Why am I so stupid?"

"I'm such a loser. I can never be like my brother."

"I can't believe I failed that test! That question was so simple! I studied it like five times!"

"Why am I like this? I can't do anything right ... "

"I hate this."

"I don't want to do this anymore ... "

Are any of these thoughts relatable? Even if you don't think this, I am almost positive you may have heard it from others. It could be your parents, siblings, friends, or even your partner. How did I know about these thoughts? It's because I have heard them so many times over 33 years of my life.

Every night, I agonized over a new circumstance that happened to me that made me feel nothing but shame, guilt, and utter defeat. I spent endless nights arguing with myself about why I was not the problem and why it was so "stupid" that I had to deal with anything.

Can any of you understand these pains? These thoughts? For those who preach, "You just need to think better!" Do you remember these feelings? These are the real feelings of those who interact with you. These feelings are what you could be truly feeling inside, too. That is why you keep encountering so many "Debbie Downers." They were always a reflection of what you truly feel.

This is what it means to embody what you feel and not what you think. It is the same thing as when you want money. When you need to pay bills, you feel desperate and start praying or "manifesting" more money. In this dire circumstance, you forget that the reason you needed money was because of these feelings. They root so deeply inside you that even when you have money, it falls through your fingers like it never existed.

This is where a perpetual cycle continues, and you will always feel like you need more.

Of course, I understand this desperation very well, too. I spent most of my young adult years working relentlessly at my jobs. There were times when I took on two jobs just to make ends meet, as if having one wasn't draining enough. I recall those moments when my moods fluctuated greatly, and I thought I was handling everything so well. Never mind that I never did anything that made me happy, which exhausted me even more. On days I was off, I would purposely cancel friend meetups, never call my family back, and never even see the light of day. Why? Because I was tired. I was tired of everything, even being awake.

My emotions ran me to the ground and fueled all my negative thoughts like a vicious cycle that made my life miserable. The irony of the situation did not dawn on me until I started seeing how much I hated surprises or any gifts in particular. I'm sure this may be confusing for some readers. Allow me to explain.

I spent most of my adult life providing for myself. After leaving the military, I had a partner and shortly broke up. It was the first time I had to get my own apartment, sustain a job, pay off a car, and so many other things—things that my mom would have taught me, I'm sure, if I stayed with her instead of leaving home at 18. However, I could not wait. I wanted to live and feel what being a "free" adult was like. I sustained myself for years and always gave amazing gifts to friends and family. I wanted to show them what it was like to be "free."

During this time, I inspired my family to branch out in many ways, and I was always proud of how they came to their own adventures. I even helped motivate some friends to obtain their college degrees and seek higher success for themselves, not just for their family. Everything was the way I had wanted it. At least, that is what I thought.

Back then, it was a deep belief of mine that if I gave more and never asked for anything, it meant I was a "good" person. In retrospect, how could I accept someone else's kindness when I never gave it to myself? Therefore, when I received something, I treated it awkwardly or, worse, it was an annoyance if it was not what I wanted. I'm sure I made some of my friends very uncomfortable during this period. Despite that, I kept going. Striving for more and always desiring more. I believed that was what I needed, and I thought I would become this amazing woman in my head if I did.

The opposite happened, though. Slowly, I started to resent the idea of being in a relationship, even when I wanted one. My demeanor with my friends started to feel more like a mask … a fragile clay mask drowning another emotion I could not name at the time. Any kindness I received made me feel so uncomfortable that I would find an excuse to run away. Honestly, I was looking for a way to run away from myself. This is why this lesson is such an important one.

As people pleasers, we lose ourselves in everyone's image or even our own image of what we believe we should be. This causes so much friction with our inner being that we feel worse at the end of the day. Therefore, I truly hope that this chapter will help you understand that you embody what you feel before what you think. This process helped me understand that it is actually our feelings that elicit our thoughts. It is instantaneous, so people believe it is more thought bound than feeling bound.

There is a huge reason for this, which I will explain more about later. However, at this time, I invite you to look at the questions below for more ways to turn your awareness on and bring back what makes you an amazing human being—the one who has so much energy and always knows how to laugh.

Lesson Two Questions

Now, I want to ask you some questions. In this section or on a separate piece of paper, try to answer the following questions:

6. When was the last time you felt truly happy? *I am talking about the moments that made you feel so good to be you, not because someone gave you a compliment or you got accolades at work. When the warmth on your skin felt most vibrant. The air in your lungs felt like sweet candy on your tongue.*

. . . .

. . . .

. . . .

. . . .

7. What were you doing that made you so happy?

. . . .

. . . .

. . . .

. . . .

8. If it has been more than six months since you felt this way, what are you feeling now?

. . . .

. . . .

. . . .

. . . .

9. Has anyone ever remarked that your emotions/thoughts are too much? And that you just need to *move on* from those emotions or thoughts?

. . . .

. . . .

. . . .

. . . .

10. How did their words make you feel? How did you want to respond to them?

. . . .

. . . .

. . . .

. . . .

11. Write down two other instances that came up recently that made you feel like you couldn't express yourself and were encouraged to be something you didn't feel like you were.

. . . .

. . . .

. . . .

. . . .

. . . .

. . . .

. . . .

. . . .

. . . .

The goal is to feel these sensations and learn the little nuances that make you feel like you and what isn't you. Allow yourself time and space to feel it. Then, allow it to unravel at its own pace. I highly recommend setting aside a time when you know you will not be disturbed and can be at true ease with the process.

Then, see if you can revisit your dream from lesson one and apply these questions to it. You'll need to tweak it, but it can apply to assess how your dream drains or invigorates you. If any discomfort arises, that is a great indicator that your alignment is off and something requires your utmost attention to be healed with love, grace, and patience.

Who Are You? I Am Me

Here it is … the big question: Who are you? Have any of you ever been asked this question? In my early adulthood, I did a lot of leadership training that included this question. Back then, I had no idea and was always quick to answer with, "I'm a Marine, I'm a daughter, a sister …" Interestingly, none of that ever felt *right*. Does this sound familiar?

Another fascinating observation I saw with this question is that not many people like or know how to talk about themselves. Many of us know how to complain about something in six different ways, but the idea of taking responsibility or owning ourselves seems to elude us. In fact, I am willing to say that even if you grabbed a stranger on the street and asked them this question in a fascinating conversation, you would find a very similar answer to the one I proposed in my early 20s. I tried this once. The poor, unsuspecting stranger almost looked at me cross-eyed for asking something so strange!

Throughout my life, I have found that many of us find safety in identifying with some kind of label. It could be a role we are in, title at work, status in life, or even political stances. At times, we become so obsessed with this need to have labels that we begin to toggle on more and more of them. It can sound something like, "*I am a daughter. My family came to the United States when I was two years old, and I am the middle sister of three. I had a distinguished honor roll in eighth grade and played four types of instruments …*" Do you see how it becomes a triage of things? It's almost like we make a timeline of our history, but it doesn't really describe us at our core.

In fact, I even asked this question to my partner in life. One night, after an intense conversation about our growth as a couple, I asked him, "Chris, who are you?" He froze and pondered that question for a long time. It was the longest moment of both our lives. After a while, he replied, "I am a son … I am a manager." I was flustered that it was his first answer. Why? In front of me was someone I admired and truly loved with all my heart. I see him in all his glory, yet he could only describe himself in small roles in his life. I can't blame him, though. Even then, I didn't have a real answer either. However, I never stopped looking for a new way to answer this question. Because I knew that deep down if I could answer this question, it wouldn't be so painful to feel so empty.

It was only later that I began to realize the importance of knowing the answer to this question. It is so easy for me to lose myself to the labels society has for me. However, they only began to ignite anxieties in me that made every moment even more unbearable than the last.

For those who do not see the issues with labels, please allow me to explain. The danger of adopting labels to answer who we are is that we lose ourselves in them. For example, my partner identified himself as a "son." This means that he consistently gave to his dad without knowing that he was causing harm to his own being by giving himself away. This can be said for parents who overidentify in their roles as well. Then, when the children leave, they are anxious and sad because there is nothing left. At least, there is nothing left inside them that gives them fulfillment. This happened to my mother each time one of us would leave home.

After seeing this develop in me and others, I reignited my journey of self-acceptance, and then, something began to change within me. Anger started to boil inside me. It wasn't anger toward myself; it was the circumstance I was in. I was tired of being tired. I was even more fed up with the idea that I had to have so many labels to be "something" in life.

After a lot of trial and error in my practice and learning my boundaries, my life started to have more vibrancy. The warmth of the sun on my skin never felt so good. The wind in my hair felt so refreshing. Even the breath I drew felt like I was rejuvenating my body. It was these moments that helped me feel deep gratitude for being me for the first time in my life. These were all new experiences that I had never felt before … and that was who I was and even am now.

This is what I was really asking when I asked: who are you? Do you even know your potential? Have you seen your real capabilities without the limitations of societal norms and expectations? What do you think you could create if you didn't have all these restrictions on you?

I am not talking about the fear, anger, guilt, or self-hate that we live in when we people please either. I wouldn't have the courage to write this book if I had those patterns playing within me. Even if they still play, I always look for new ways to chip away at them. The possibilities are endless, and how we show up in the world becomes different.

Your true self, the one that sleeps inside you, is not capable of committing a crime or anything atrocious! Sure, you will hurt some people's feelings along the way and even lose some close ones. However, I'd like to ask you this: would it be worth it if waking up another day doesn't feel like it is a horrible thing to do? Would it be worth it if you didn't have to go to bed with the worst thoughts of yourself? Would it be worth it if you no longer need to feel depressed about situations you can not change or help?

What would it take for you to want to know who you really are? I've met countless people in my life who lived in alignment and those who have not. The ones who have not, you know deep down you aren't. That is when the setbacks are always harder than the last time. That is when you feel like everything is against you, which might be the case. However, there is a better way. By knowing who you are, you unlock endless possibilities only for you. You tap into the support system of your dreams, and there, you will find the things you always wanted and the things that were wanting you all that time. Your dreams and desires are as real as your reality. It is up to you to discover the side of you that can make that happen.

Lesson Three Questions

Now, I want to ask you some questions. In this section or on a separate piece of paper, try to answer the following questions:

12. Who are you? *Your first answer is the right one. Sit with that and see what comes up. For those who answer with your name, go to point 14.*

. . . .

. . . .

. . . .

. . . .

. . . .

13. Does that answer feel authentically you? If not, does anything else come up?

. . . .

. . . .

. . . .

. . . .

. . . .

14. Did you consider your ambitions, interests, or goals in life before your name?

. . . .

. . . .

. . . .

. . . .

15. Where in your body feels out of place or uncomfortable with this question?

. . . .

. . . .

. . . .

. . . .

. . . .

16. Did this question elicit any memories? If so, which ones?

. . . .

. . . .

. . . .

. . . .

. . . .

   a. What did that memory show you?

. . . .

. . . .

. . . .

. . . .

   b. Where did you feel like you stopped being you, and a shadow of you emerged?

. . . .

. . . .

. . . .

. . . .

c.   What did you really want to do at that time instead?

. . . .

. . . .

. . . .

. . . .

The goal here is to feel your way into these sensations. This is not to justify what you think or feel. A friendly reminder that this is not a blame game either. This practice is about you accepting all that occurs. Therefore, sitting with discomfort is a way for you to surrender into this flow. Acceptance is the key to coming home. Home to you. Where you always belonged.

Give yourself grace. The observations you had up until this point were not the easiest to digest. However, with love, understanding, and patience for yourself, it will become easier and less enormous.

Be Like a Tree and Leave Out All the Rest

What is a tree? Some may think of a big tree standing strong and tall against a city landscape. Others may think of how resilient the tree is because no matter how much we cut it down, it keeps trying to grow again. The interesting part is I am not talking about any of this.

My point is that most trees start as a seed. They have to bide their time and find the right resources to grow and thrive. Every tree has to start small at one point or another. Depending on its environment, it can grow faster because of competition; however, that does not mean it has to be anything other than itself.

The tree does not stop searching for light or anything it needs to sustain itself. It doesn't forget that its roots are as important as the light. Its core always knew what it needed to thrive. So, my biggest question for you is: why can't you remember how to thrive?

I've spent my entire life yearning and running after acceptance from other human beings. I forgot that I needed to fulfill my needs and wants first. Worst of all, I could not even forgive myself when I made unwarranted mistakes or bad decisions. This made me fall into a vicious cycle of wanting to meet other's expectations and perceptions of me instead. The dire need to be important and greed for acceptance started to cultivate traits that did not serve me, people pleasing being one of them.

In my earlier lessons, I said how I took care of my big office without rest and food. At that time, I felt that if I provided all they needed, they would take care of me in the same way. It was based on an assumption and wanting to guilt others into pleasing me. However, most of the time they disappointed me. That continuous hurt was really painful. Does this scenario resonate with anyone? This is a perfect example of how I forgot how to thrive.

There were other moments as well. When I was a pre-teen, I was asked to babysit my siblings often. There were six of us, myself included, and it was a tall order for someone so young. However, I did it because I wanted to help my busy single mom, who worked seven days a week to support us. I wanted to help where I could and always did my best. There were days when that felt amazing—the chores were all done, I got the kids to do all their homework, and the house was spick-and-span clean.

Then, there were some awful days when I didn't want to get up. I didn't do any chores, and the kids did not do their homework, and the house was an utter mess. Of course, that is when my depression hit me like a ton of bricks. And then, my mom would say awful things to me and make me feel even worse for not being of any help to her.

This was the last thing I wanted. Especially when I did well, my mom never said any kind words of encouragement. On bad days, the treatment got worse, and she would sometimes even ignore me. This hurt a lot, as you can imagine. No child would like to know that their mother thought of them as so unreliable or pathetic. The ache in my chest and choking sensations in my throat throbbed for a long time.

It took me years to understand that I masked the pain with indifference because my mother never accepted any negative emotions from me. She was so busy being strong for us all that she forgot that she was expecting a child not to be, well ... a child. My tears were unacceptable, and my love for her was never enough because, at that time, I wasn't enough no matter what I did to please or help her.

As days passed and my duties as one of the eldest children increased, I accepted these responsibilities with the hope that she would see me and love me for all I did. That was not the case, unfortunately. One responsibility multiplied to eight more. The more I took, the worse it got. I started to feel frustrated and angry at her. Why? Because on the days that I completed all the tasks, I was not praised or acknowledged. On the days that I missed one task, she made sure I felt like the worst disappointment in her life. Crazy enough ... This followed me throughout my life as well. This cycle with partners and all I held dear ... Can anyone understand that?

Before any of you judge, please know that I love and adore my mother. This is a story that ruled my life until I understood her deep love for me. I invite you to think of a scenario where this or something similar has happened to you. Or better yet, can you feel into yourself right now? What did this story make you feel? Where do you feel that sensation?

Again, the goal is not to blame anyone, my scenario, or even yourself. Your goal here is to remember and feel that moment for what it was. Where does it come up in your body? Is it a rock on your chest? A lump stuck in your throat? Is your mid-back aching? Is your lower back pinching?

Those are great indicators that your body is telling you the story of when you got lost. You imprinted those harsh moments into yourself and have been carrying them with you all this time. I am here to tell you this is just energy. You are safe now. You are loved now. You are appreciated now. Even if no one comes up when you say that, you should know it is you. You are loving and appreciating yourself by doing this practice.

Great job. You are doing so great!

It's Okay To Be Stuck. It's Not Okay To Stay Stuck

"I always wonder why birds choose to stay in the same place when they can fly anywhere on the earth, then I ask myself the same question."

–Harun Yahya

Continuing from the previous chapter, you are *NOT* a tree. You can adopt its way of being, but you are not it. You are a living, breathing *human* being. Something my beloved grandfather once told me was, "You are alive. Why don't you act like it?"

You see, this chapter is all about the power of choice. Being alive means you get to choose. You can choose to be unhappy or super happy. You can choose to let all the things that have been coming up for you rule your life, or you can allow it to pass. There were plenty of times when I felt stuck metaphorically and physically speaking. I was stuck at jobs that made me feel less than and never gave me a chance to grow. I was stuck in relationships that did not make me happy or accepted. I was stuck in my relationship with my family, not knowing if we would ever understand each other.

These are real moments and fears that I had and sometimes still confront to this day. I can vividly remember going to work at my jobs and feeling the same doom and gloom as anybody else. It was pretty much the same thing all day: the same complaints, the same people making them, the same office, the same events, and it got boring. I was tired of going in to do the same work. I was tired of having no exciting projects. I was tired of seeing nothing but the same old people. Nothing made me feel alive or new.

This is, of course, the safer version of what is out there. I've had my experiences with toxic work environments as well. In one instance, I was in a role that required me to do account receivables. I was the only one for the entire department. Some days were busier than others, and I was always looking for a new way to be of use to my ever-busy co-workers. In fact, I even went out of my way to be responsible for planning welcoming events for new employees (we had a high turnover) and goodbye events for them, too. Then, I took on managing our supplies for the office and training people on my roles.

I never thought much about what I did until we got a job evaluation to fill out. They wanted us to list all the things we did in the office. At first, I took the recommendations of my supervisor and wrote down things that were only relevant to my role. However, one of my friends told me not to. It was a good thing that I didn't listen to my supervisor because when the final review was done, it turned out my role had more duties than all the other roles in the office. It was then that I found I was performing only second to the supervisor. Crazy, huh?

Here is the biggest kicker, though: they never wanted me to do the other people's work. Back then, I was bitter. I was mad that I was passed over for learning more. The environment was already stifling, and I didn't get what I wanted. Then, it turned out to be the best thing that ever happened to me. When I left that role, after a while, they demoted the responsibilities and no one ever filled the role with the same responsibilities again. At least, that is what I heard. I could totally be wrong.

So, the real moral of the story is to understand that your "stuck" may just be a choice. It could feel crazily scary now, but what are the chances it could be better than you ever imagined? That is why I practice these lessons daily. You are meant to embody these feelings and allow them to release in their own time. Once you are done releasing them, the choice in front of you won't feel so daunting. I am not saying you won't feel the fear. There is always some form of trepidation, but there will also be an underlying sense of faith: faith in yourself and that what happens next will only benefit you and others, just like the experience I shared with you. I didn't get to see the end, but it came back around.

You are more than capable of doing this as well. I believe in you!

Lesson Five Questions

Now, I want to ask you some questions!

17. Where in your life do you see yourself being "stuck"?

. . . .

. . . .

. . . .

. . . .

18. Are you choosing to be stuck, or is it just a façade because you are scared to make a choice?

. . . .

. . . .

. . . .

. . . .

19. Does this choice impact anyone else?

. . . .

. . . .

. . . .

. . . .

a.   Who is it impacting, and what consequences may arise from this person being impacted?

. . . .

. . . .

. . . .

b. How might it be different if they were not impacted by your choice?

. . . .

. . . .

. . . .

. . . .

c. Who are you really trying to please by not making the choice?

. . . .

. . . .

. . . .

. . . .

Accepting the sensations that come up in your body as you answer these questions will allow it to pass and roll out of your body, allowing space for you and the endless possibilities to come in.

Love Your Mind, but Love Your Heart First

And here, we have the final lesson. This is a beautiful chapter, and I am so glad you made it here. In our current world, everyone focuses on the mind and how everything has to make sense.

May I challenge this quickly, though? Miracles happen every day! Scientists can't explain them all, and many amazing spiritual practitioners have their own explanations. However, this isn't a topic about who is right and who is wrong. This is more to acknowledge that your mind and heart are powerful enablers for you in this life.

Your mind helps you build tangible steps toward impossible goals, while your heart will light your way even when setbacks happen. How could you not love both? How can you choose one or the other? They are so wonderful and amazing to have, scientifically and more!

Earlier in the book, I mentioned how we are how we feel and not what we think. This chapter is all about knowing that your heart knows the way, just like when you decide it is better to end a relationship that no longer brings you joy or leave a job that makes you feel less than what you are worth. Your heart was always lighting the way for you. Even when you were scared, it helped you hurdle all obstacles.

Don't underestimate your heart. It is the key to this practice and the guide that helps you find the joy that you denied yourself for so long. It is a testament that you are alive. Allowing yourself to feel your way in life is a great thing.

In fact, I recall the first time I ever listened to my heart. It told me that I could join the military and I would be able to leave my home. Up to that date, no one had ever left home successfully. My older sister tried and was not successful. Therefore, I knew if I wanted to live the life of my dreams, I needed to leave. So, I did the impossible at that point. I was 17 and told my mom to sign the enlistment papers, or I would sign them at 18, and she would not see me anymore. I was terrified of what she would say. I was such a "good" girl up until that point. She was so angry with me ... but I got my wish. For those in traditional Asian households, I'm sure you understand that this was the most unconventional path ever!

I cried when I left that fateful day. I cried so badly because it was the first time I had ever left home, and it was the first time I ever saw my mother collapse, crying that her baby was leaving her. Three months is a long time after all. Imagine a young 18-year-old watching her proud mother collapse in front of her because her daughter was really leaving. Even though it was not permanent, she didn't know how long it would be until she would see me again. The odds of me failing were pretty high too.

The funniest thing happened, though. I was the slowest runner in my platoon and was threatened with being "dropped" (recycled to another platoon) often, which would delay my graduation date and extend my time away from my family.

However, my heart never failed me. Every day, it reignited my faith that I would pass and see my family again soon. Like a miracle, I made it to the end with my original group. May I remark that when we first started, there were 102 women, and by graduation, there were only about 40 of us. More than half were not from the original group either. I'm sure no one in my platoon ever knew how many nights I prayed fervently to pass so I could see my family again. It was that desire that drove me to the end. Even when my body was ready to crumble and my mind no longer worked, I persevered.

This is the power of your heart. This is the power of you. Embrace your heart. It is beautifully delicate and strong in its own way. It is the motivation behind all your desires and the beauty you see in life. Please understand that without your heart, nothing would have the luster that it has. That and this embodiment practice would be nothing.

Besides, you made it this far with mostly your mind working. Why not try embracing the heart and see how it goes? Can you imagine how amazing it can turn out!?

Lesson Six Questions

20. What has your heart been leading you toward lately?

. . . .

. . . .

. . . .

. . . .

. . . .

. . . .

. . . .

21. When do you feel its prodding? *I am not talking about unhealthy obsessions either such as contacting an ex that hurt you physically, mentally, and emotionally. I am talking about when you feel the need to take action for something you feel inspired to do.*

. . . .

. . . .

. . . .

. . . .

. . . .

. . . .

. . . .

Conclusion

That was a lot to unpack! Well done. You finished. I congratulate you because some of the stuff that came up may not be easy to process. It was difficult for me even while I was proofreading this after an editor! However, by finishing, you really did something amazing. You unearthed things that would have drowned you in a sea of self-perpetuating misery if you had not found them. They are the undercurrents that played through your life while you were busy living. Now that you have brought them up to the surface, you can see them for what they are and not as who you are. This is important.

It is important to know that you are not the victim of any story. You are a co-creator. Co-creators had horrible things happen to them. However, they never allowed themselves to be limited by that experience. This is why we fall in love with the idea of heroes and villains to begin with. They embody the bravery and acceptance that we all hope to feel! The best part is that you can now embark on the journey of being your own hero/villian, whichever you prefer. Only you can fill your glass. Only you can see the world through the lens of blessings … because you are the real gift that came into it. A lot of times, we forget that we aren't the ones making space for the world. It's the world that is making space for us. That is how important you are to this reality.

Just your existence right now gives hope to another person. Why? Because you are lighting yourself up on this journey home. As you come home to yourself, you will see that everything is already perfect the way it is. And if you aren't happy with something, well, that is because you are powerful enough to make that change that you want to occur. It is perfect because you are already perfect. Perfectly imperfect.

Have faith in yourself on this journey. It is the real journey when your life really begins, which reminds me that I never told you who I am. I would like to share that with you now as we part because it took me 34 years to write this. Every word came from my heart to yours, and it is my highest hope that it will light up your soul. That way, you can pass the light on … Hope is never lost on those willing to find it.

Who am I?

I am me. The one who loves all aspects of me. The me who lived through hard times as well as beautiful times. All are as unforgettable as the last. I am the me who achieved unimaginable dreams and inspired many in their wake. I am wholesomely and wonderfully me in all my ugly and pretty. I choose to be me every day and help others see the beauty in being them as well. That is who I am! I am Victoria Tran and Chien Thang Thi Nguyen.

About the Author

Victoria Tran is an embodiment coach and business owner, whose background spanned from government to the corporate world in logistics. She has always been passionate about helping those around her excel and expand while forgetting her own accomplishments.

There were some incredible moments in her life that happened that she was numb toward and quickly moved on from. When she got into a big car accident in January 2023, the iceberg (her frozen life) started to collapse. This is when she quit her stable job later that year, after realizing how unsatisfied she was with her work. Despite all her massive contributions to the workforce, she embarked on her entrepreneurship in 2023 to finally feel the happiness and freedom she yearned for deeply in her soul.

This was the year she discovered a healing process that allowed her to feel and create the happiest moments of her life. Her motto in life is, *"The biggest hurdles in life are mostly ourselves. Only when we finally understand and accept them can we really empower ourselves to set the stage for our biggest breakthroughs."*

Now, she is a co-owner of a business with her amazing partner in life and business, Christopher Martinez. Their goal is to help bring humanity back into the world of technology through the lens of healing and human-led sales approaches to help them boldly communicate the value of what they're creating and confidently sell it.

On the side, she helps lead a women-led community that empowers others to become the most powerful versions of themselves, while creating the most beautiful chapters of their lives.

If you feel compelled to work with Victoria, please connect with her on LinkedIn:

www.linkedin.com/in/victoria-tran27
www.linkedin.com/company/startupsnt/

Acknowledgments

I want to say a deep thank you to everything that has made this book come to life. First, I wanted to thank my beloved partner, Christopher Martinez. The man who unexpectedly came into my life and changed everything. This book would not have happened without his love and support. From the bottom of my heart, I am so grateful to you, and I am so happy that you have chosen me to spend forever with!

I want to express my deep gratitude to Ekaterina Sky, the passionate artist and conservationist I have come to love and adore for all her work in her communities. She graciously accepted my request to create the artwork for this book, despite being swamped with tight deadlines. I am ever grateful that she took on my project and delivered the magic that only she and her team could provide.

I want to ensure I give credit to an amazing quantum energy healer as well. Paget Kagy helped me with her practice, which started me down this path of healing. Her practice helped me create my own style and gave birth to this book formally. It was thanks to this incredible healer that I can share so many of my stories all with you.

I want to thank God and my angels for this beautiful journey. There were lots of times when I wanted to give up and was at the edge ... however, with their patience, love, and guidance, I came to what I was meant to be.

I am grateful for myself. I had to write the book with my guides and my body. Therefore, I deserve a big thank you as well!

Thank you to my incredible mother and sisters. Our earlier life was challenging, as many others are. Despite that, you've continued to shower me with love, support, and, at times, understanding for all my wanton ways.

I want to thank my pets, Annie and Benjamin (Benji). Through my healing process, they were with me. Mostly Annie because she is primarily my dog. We've been through a lot together, and I could not imagine any other pet than her on this path.

Last but not least, I wanted to thank Mariam Arcana, who is not only a gifted spiritualist but also a gifted editor with immense creativity who blessed this book with her review.